Proclaim
My
Feasts

• • • •

DeAnna Willman

Proclaim My Feasts

DeAnna Willman
Distributed by Smashwords
Copyright 2017 DeAnna Willman
Seven Lamps Ministries
Cover artwork copyright 2014 Gail Andrews
Used by permission of Gail Andrews

No portion of this book may be digitally or photo copied without written permission from the author. However, the facts, scriptures, and understanding from the scriptures found in this book can be used frequently and as needed. Remember to take EVERYTHING back to scripture. God's word is the ultimate authority in everything.

The scripture quotations found in this book are taken from the Holy Bible, New International Version. Copyright 1973, 1978, 1984 by International Bible Society. Used by permission of Zondervan Publishing House.

For my children and grandchildren
who are truly a precious treasure from our King.
May this be a lasting legacy as I proclaim
to the generations to come the goodness
of our King.

Introduction

I admit that I am an oddity among most Christians. From a very early age I began reading the bible from end to end several times a year. I did my own study of scriptures even as a young kid. As I developed into a young adult I began seeking in scripture understanding beyond bible studies and weekly sermons. Along with this trait came the tendency to question everything, including everything I learned at church. There is much that I learned at church to which I still hold. Everything that passed the test of whether or not it was found and supported in scripture, how it measured with what God specifically told us, and if it honors my Messiah (in his eyes) is still a firm part of my belief today. However, there is also much that failed those tests and is no longer a part of my belief. This book is part of what I have had to relearn.

The apostle Paul wrote to Timothy that we are all to study to show ourselves approved to YHWH. At the time that he wrote those words, there was no "new testament." What Paul was telling Timothy to study was what the church calls the "old testament." The apostle Paul was also able to reason with Jews and gentiles alike showing that Yeshua was the Messiah from the scriptures- the "old testament". Paul did not have the book of John to hand out to people in order to bring them to salvation. Our Messiah, himself, told people that if they did not believe the things written by Moses, they would not believe in Him. These things motivated within me a deeper study of the "old testament".

It is within this deeper, purposeful study that the Holy Spirit began revealing things to me that are wonderful and have brought me to a closer relationship with my God and King. It would be much too long of a book to share all that I have learned and continue to learn. So, I have chosen to simply share with you what the Spirit has revealed to me concerning the feasts that I had been taught were only for the Jews, or had been made obsolete. I pray that it will bless you, but more than that, I pray that this book will motivate you to also dig deeper into the part of scriptures that speaks of our Messiah before he ever arrived on this earth.

May YHWH bless you and keep you.

DeAnna Willman

Throughout this book you will find that I use the Hebrew name for God (YHWH/YHVH) as this is the name God instructed Moses to use. I also use the name Yeshua for our Messiah (Jesus) as this is what he was actually called by his mother and those who knew him while He walked this earth.

Chapter 1

Sabbath

YHWH said to Moses, "Speak to the Israelites and say to them: 'These are my appointed feasts, the appointed feasts of YHWH, which you are to proclaim as sacred assemblies.' " Leviticus 23:1-2

I grew up in the church for most of my life. I was there from the time I was a week old and attended nearly every time the doors were open, even into the early years of my marriage. I had been taught by the church that the feasts described in Exodus, Leviticus, and Deuteronomy were only for the Jews, or that they had been done away with at Yeshua's death on the cross. For many years I believed this doctrine without question.

A certain event that was in the news in the early part of this century prompted me to question the removal of the Sabbath from the life of believers. I began studying out the Sabbath from scripture and was very surprised to find that it is mentioned over 150 times in the whole bible. From beginning to end this special day is mentioned over and over again. This fact made me realize that this is a very important topic, one that a believer should definitely understand in order to "show yourself approved."

Why do I start with the Sabbath when I talk about the feasts? It is the very first thing/day in all creation that YHWH declares holy, (Genesis 2:1-3) and it is the first day listed when YHWH gave Moses the list of feasts that were to be observed by the Israelites (Leviticus 23:3). It is the one feast listed that is weekly, rather than just yearly. And, I figure if it is at the beginning of YHWH's list, it should be the first one on our list as well.

Sabbath was the seventh day of creation week. As a result, it is always the seventh day of the week. YHWH declared it was holy, set apart from all other days (Genesis 2:3). Later He declares that it is set apart for Him and for His set apart people (Exodus 20:8-11; Exodus 31:12-17; Leviticus 23:3; Deuteronomy 5:12-15). Nearly 2000 years later, our Messiah stated the same thing concerning his Sabbath (Mark 2:27).

Throughout the scriptures, the prophets were sent to Israel to call them back to YHWH before they experienced His judgment. Of the many sins that YHWH listed each time a prophet went forth, the defilement of His Sabbath is the most repeated of all other sins (Nehemiah 13:15-22; Isaiah 56:2,6; 58:13; Jeremiah 17:21-27; Lamentations 1:7; 2:6; Ezekiel 20:12-24; 22:8,26; Amos 8:5). Those prophets also spoke of a kingdom to come when our Messiah returns to reign on this earth. In those prophecies it is noted that the Sabbath will be observed by YHWH's people in the kingdom of our Messiah (Isaiah 66:23; Ezekiel 44:24; 45:17; 46:1-12).

Our Messiah was the Word of YHWH made in flesh. He walked out before our eyes what the torah (God's instructions) looked like and what it meant. He did as his Father commanded and is one with the very God who made the Sabbath holy. He observed the Sabbath as meant by YHWH. He rested, encouraged others to rest, met with other believers, taught the scriptures, and healed the sick -physically and spiritually. Nothing he did or said was contrary or contradictory to what YHWH instructed in the scriptures regarding His Sabbath (Matthew 12; Mark 1:21; 2:23-28; 3:2-4; 6:2; Luke 4:16, 31;

John 7:22; 9:14-16). Not once did Yeshua declare the Sabbath obsolete or only for the Jews. In fact, in his prophecies concerning the end times just before his second coming, he makes it clear he expects his disciples will still be keeping the Sabbath (Matthew 24: 20).

Next, I found that the apostles also kept the Sabbath even after the resurrection and ascension of Yeshua (Matthew 28:1; Mark 15:42; 16:1; Luke 23:54-56; John 19:31; Acts 13:14-44; 15:21; 16:13; 17:2; 18:4). On the Sabbath they were meeting in synagogues, or in other places of prayer for Jews who did not live in cities with synagogues. They were meeting in the temple. They were reasoning with others and teaching the good news about Yeshua on the Sabbath. Nothing about our Messiah's life, death, and resurrection changed the Sabbath or the instructions from YHWH concerning His special day.

Not one word from Genesis to Revelation changes the Sabbath day or makes it obsolete. In all of my study and research I could not find one instance in scripture where YHWH or Yeshua changed or did away with the Sabbath (Matthew 5:17-20). Add that to the fact that YHWH declared it was to be a sign between Him and His people forever, and the fact that the prophets spoke of the Sabbath being observed in the future kingdom, I had to rethink my belief surrounding this day (Exodus 31:12-17: Isaiah 66:23).

Later I found that it was the Catholic Church and Emperor Constantine who jointly decreed that the Sabbath was no longer relevant, and that Sunday was to be the day of worship for the believer. This is well documented in the Catholic Church records, lessons, doctrines, and newsletters. This is also acknowledged by many non- Catholic church leaders in their writings, lessons, sermons, and doctrines. Yet, this man-made doctrine has been taught in the church of all denominations for the last 1800 years.

Once I realized that the instructions and expectations of YHWH concerning His Sabbath were still relevant to His people, I began looking into how to observe this special day. Was my Sabbath to look like that of the Orthodox Jews? Or was it something else? What specifically did YHWH instruct and what does it look like for us?

Then YHWH said to Moses, "I will rain down bread from heaven for you. The people are to go out each day and gather enough for that day. In this way I will test them and see whether they will follow my instructions. On the sixth day they are to prepare what they bring in, and that is to be twice as much as they gather on the other days." (Exodus 16:4-5).

Exodus 16 is the first place YHWH gives His people specific instructions regarding the Sabbath. YHWH told His people He would give them bread each day, except on the seventh day of the week. That day was to be a day of rest, even for Him. He would not provide bread that day, but would provide enough bread on the sixth day for the Israelites to gather extra and have enough for the Sabbath as well. Those who obeyed had bread to eat on the Sabbath. Those who disobeyed went hungry. Nevertheless, some of the people went out on the seventh day to gather it, but they found none.

Then YHWH said to Moses, "How long will my people refuse to keep my commands and my instructions? Bear in mind that YHWH has given you the Sabbath; that is why on the sixth day he gives you bread for two days. " (Exodus 16:27-30)

It is obvious from this chapter that one is not to spend Sabbath providing, seeking, or cooking food. That is to be done the day before so that the Sabbath can be a day of rest; a day of rest for the breadwinner in the family, and a day of rest for the one who usually does the preparing of meals. YHWH promised to provide enough on the day before so that His people will be able to prepare it and have plenty left for eating on the Sabbath.

"Remember the Sabbath day by keeping it holy. Six days you shall labor and do all your work, but the seventh day is a Sabbath to YHWH your God. On it you shall not do any work, neither you, nor your son, nor daughter, nor your manservant or maidservant, nor our animals nor the alien within your gates. For in six days YHWH made the heavens and the earth, the sea, and all that is in them, but He rested on the seventh day. Therefore, YHWH blessed the Sabbath day and made it holy." (Exodus 20:8-11)

This is our next set of instructions for the Sabbath. YHWH clearly tells us to work on the first six days of the week, but to rest from our work on the Sabbath. For those in the workforce that means that you do your business Sunday through Friday, but do not work or engage in business on the day we call Saturday. For the housewife, it means that she is to do her work of cooking, cleaning, and maintaining a wonderful home Sunday through Friday. On Sabbath there is to be rest for her. For those who employ servants such as maids, gardeners, cooks, etc., you may employ their services Sunday through Friday. On Saturday you are to give them rest. For the rest of us, it means that we do not make anyone work for us on the Sabbath. This includes clerks, servers, repair men, shop keepers, hair dressers, business owners, babysitters, and unless it is an emergency, even doctors and nurses. Anyone who might serve you in any capacity is be allowed a day of rest from serving or working for you.

Now, in an emergency, it is perfectly acceptable to go to a hospital or doctor. All of torah speaks to life and mercy. Therefore, if one's health or very life is at stake, it is acceptable to seek help (Matthew 12:1-14). Just know that YHWH wants you, your family, those who serve you, even your animals to have a rest on the Sabbath.

Exodus 31:12-17 expounds upon this with a slight emphasis on how important the day is to YHWH. It is here that YHWH also tells His people that the Sabbath is His sign or mark upon those who are His. One might equate this to a wedding ring worn by a bride. Just as we know that anti-messiah has a mark to be taken by his followers, our King also has a mark to be taken by His followers; His Sabbath.

In Numbers 15 we have an example of someone failing to keep the Sabbath holy. Verses 32-35 tell us the incident of a man who was stoned to death because he had been collecting sticks on the Sabbath. These verses immediately follow YHWH's instructions regarding rebellion.

"But anyone who sins defiantly, whether native born or alien, blasphemes YHWH and that person must be cut off from his people. Because he has despised YHWH's word and broken His commands, that person must surely be cut off; his guilt remains on him." (Numbers 15:30-31)

It is here that Moses included the incident about a man who was collecting sticks on the Sabbath. It was implied that this man had been walking in rebellion. That was apparently not his first and only time of defiling the Sabbath. It was also indicated within the Hebrew language here that the man was gathering the wood with intent to do something with it that would entail work. That was not a mere case of a man who needed firewood to keep warm, or a man who sinned once. Yeshua did not teach us anything new, but in Matthew 18 he reminded the disciples how they were supposed to deal with the sin of a brother. This very "formula" was originally established in the Torah and would have been carried out in regard to one who was sinning.

We have to conclude from the incident recorded that the man was walking in rebellion and refused to repent. His actions were blasphemy against YHWH and made it clear that he did not desire to return to a relationship with YHWH. Therefore, he was stoned to death.

This section of scripture teaches a few more things about how to keep the Sabbath holy. All of Torah is about life and mercy. If the man's life or another person's life were in danger there would be mercy toward any "work" on the Sabbath. However, the man was about doing what he wanted, when he wanted, as he wanted. He was putting himself above honoring and meeting with YHWH. If we are seeking to honor and please YHWH in our keeping of the Sabbath, it will be evident in our behavior. If we are doing it simply because it is commanded, or to keep from getting into trouble, it displeases and dishonors our King. We will be no better than the people of Israel who were sent into exile for their sin (Amos 8:5).

Leviticus 23:3 reads, "There are six days when you may work, but the seventh day is a Sabbath of rest, a day of sacred assembly. You are not to do any work; wherever you live, it is a Sabbath to YHWH."

Here we find our next instruction on how to observe the Sabbath. It is a day of sacred assembly. Some bibles call it "holy convocation." The Sabbath is a day of meeting together with other believers just as we witnessed Yeshua and the disciples doing. The word convocation means "a rehearsal". What is rehearsed? Though they may not be aware of it, those who keep the Sabbath are rehearsing some of the very rest we will experience in the Kingdom of our Messiah.

The prophecies regarding the coming Kingdom are glorious! They speak of peace and rest that has never before been known on this planet. It will be 1000 years of being with our Messiah, learning the Torah from his own lips, ruling and reigning with him, and taking the gospel to every corner of the earth. There will be no war. We will own land and eat from what we bring forth from the earth. We will be praising and worshiping our King continually. The Sabbath is just a shadow of this amazing time to come! Each time we keep the Sabbath and meet with other believers we are rehearsing this yet unfulfilled prophecy.

Actors and musicians will rehearse a piece over and over and over again until they have it perfected. They do so in order that they might be in the right place at the right time doing the right thing. It is the same with us who keep the Sabbath, and all the feasts, for that matter. We are rehearsing what will be taking place so that we can be in the right place, at the right time, doing the right thing. We will be prepared for the things that will take place according to YHWH's time table.

Deuteronomy 5 is basically Moses' retelling of the Ten Words that the Israelites heard spoken from the mountain by YHWH. Many English bibles call them the Ten Commandments. The fourth word is again to keep the Sabbath holy. However, in verse 15, YHWH adds a new facet to the Sabbath.

"Remember that you were slaves in Egypt and that YHWH your Elohim (God) brought you out of there with a mighty hand and an outstretched arm. Therefore, YHWH your Elohim has commanded you to observe the Sabbath."

First, we were told that we were to observe the Sabbath because YHWH rested on it and made it holy. Now we find that we are also to observe it in order to remember our slavery in Egypt. For those of this on this side of the Exodus with Moses, that means that we are to remember our bondage to sin (Egypt) and how YHWH redeemed us from it. Because of that redemption we are to observe the Sabbath and keep it holy.

In the book of Jeremiah YHWH was spelling out the sins of Judah and calling them to repentance. In chapter 17, verses 21-27 we find that the people of Judah were buying and selling wares on the Sabbath. YHWH told them, through Jeremiah, that if they would stop doing business and return to the delight of His Sabbath, He would protect and prosper the country. If, however, they continued to choose to do their own thing on the Sabbath and defile YHWH's holy day, He would bring judgment in the form of destruction of Judah. Not only did the people go into exile, but all the cities were destroyed. There was nothing left of the kingdom of Judah.

After the Jews were allowed to return to the region of Judah, Nehemiah found a similar situation. In chapter 10, Nehemiah put a stop to the buying and selling of wares on the Sabbath. Yet, when he returned to Jerusalem several years later (Chapter 13), Nehemiah found that the people had gone back to buying and selling on the Sabbath. Nehemiah chastised the people and prayed for YHWH to forgive the people. He was well aware that defiling the Sabbath was blasphemy against YHWH. It broke his heart to find the people once again doing their own thing and breaking the Sabbath.

From these two prophets we can determine that buying and selling on the Sabbath, whether or not it has to do with your own work, is not keeping the Sabbath holy. In a sense, purchasing and selling are the means of providing what your family needs or wants. We are to rest in the provision of YHWH on the Sabbath. Purchasing also induces another to work on our behalf. We are not to make anyone work for us on the Sabbath.

The prophet Isaiah was speaking to the whole house of Israel when he spoke the words of YHWH.

"This is what YHWH says, 'Maintain justice and do what is right, for my salvation is close at hand and my righteousness will soon be revealed.

Blessed is the man who does this, the man who holds it fast, who keeps the Sabbath without desecrating it, and keeps his hand from doing any evil... To the eunuchs who keep my Sabbaths, who choose what pleases me and hold fast to my covenant- to them I will give within my temple and its walls a memorial and a name better than sons or daughters; I will give them an everlasting name that will not be cut off. And foreigners who bind themselves to YHWH to serve Him, to love the name of YHWH and to worship him, all who keep the Sabbath without desecrating it and who hold fast to my covenant- these I will bring to my holy mountain and give them joy in my house of prayer. " (Isaiah 56:1-8)

"If you keep your feet from breaking the Sabbath and from doing as you please on my holy day, if you call the Sabbath a delight and YHWH's holy day honorable, and if you honor it by not going your own way and not doing as you please or speaking

PROCLAIM MY FEASTS 17

idle words, then you will find your joy in YHWH, and I will cause you to ride on the heights of the land and to feast on the inheritance of your father Jacob,' The mouth of YHWH has spoken." (Isaiah 58:13-14)

In Deuteronomy Moses told the people of YHWH that he had laid before them blessings and curses, life and death. He encouraged them to choose life and blessings by being obedient. YHWH promised life and blessings to those who love and obey Him, including the keeping of His Sabbath. He promised it again through the prophets, specifically through Isaiah. It is HIS holy day and He has given it to HIS people.

We have looked at the instructions that YHWH gave concerning keeping HIS Sabbath holy. They are simple. From sundown Friday night to sundown Saturday night, you are to:

1. REST
2. Do no regular work
3. Don't make others work for you
4. Make the day separate and different from the other 6 days
5. Meet with YHWH and His people
6. Remember (creation and redemption) and rehearse (future kingdom peace and rest)

Anything else you do to make the day special is up to you. Just know that traditions are special when they help you enjoy and honor the day, but they are never to be placed equal to or above what YHWH has stated in His Word. He never commanded the lighting of candles or prayer shawls or dancing or challah bread. Those things are nice and can be very special.

They are only traditions. They are not required nor should anyone expect them of anyone else keeping the Sabbath.

May your observance of YHWH's holy day bring you blessing and bring honor to our King!

ב

Chapter 2

Passover

After my family started keeping the Sabbath for several months, the Spirit stirred within us the desire to study out the rest of His feasts. I do not believe it coincidental that this was a short time before the very first yearly feast on YHWH's calendar was upon us; Passover. The first instructions regarding Passover are found in Exodus 12. Some of the instructions in that chapter deal specifically with the first Passover, the one that took place just before the Exodus of the Hebrews from Egypt. However, there are many instructions included that pertain to every Passover. Let's take a look.

YHWH said to Moses and Aaron, "This month is to be for you the first month, the first month of your year. Tell the whole community of Israel that on the tenth day of this month each man is to take a lamb for his family, one for each household. If any household is too small for a whole lamb, they must share one with their nearest neighbor, having taken into account the number of people there are. You are to determine the amount of lamb needed in accordance with what each person will eat. The animals you choose must be year old males without defect, and you may take them from the sheep or goats. Take care of them until the fourteenth of the month when all the people of the community of Israel must slaughter them at twilight. Then they are to take some of the blood and put in on the sides and tops of the doorframes of the houses where they eat the lambs. That same night they are to eat the meat roasted over the fire, along with bitter herbs, and bread made without yeast. Do not eat the meat raw or cooked in water, but roast it over the fire- head, legs, and inner parts. Do not leave any part of it till morning; if some is left till morning, you must burn it. This is how you are to eat it; with your cloak tucked into your belt, your sandals on your feet, and your staff in hand. Eat it in haste; it is YHWH's Passover." (Exodus 12:1-11)

First, YHWH determined the beginning of the year by telling Moses that it was to be 14 days before Passover. That time of year falls between the months we call March and April. On the tenth day of that month, each family was to select a year-old male sheep or goat without blemish. It was to be brought into the home and taken care of in order to keep it free from blemish. On the fourteenth day of the month, the sheep or goats were to be slaughtered at twilight, the meat roasted over a fire, and eaten that night with bitter herbs and unleavened bread.

"Obey these instructions as a lasting ordinance for you and your descendants. When you enter the land that YHWH will give you as He promised, observe this service. And when your children ask you, 'What does this service mean to you?' then tell them, 'It is the Passover sacrifice to YHWH who passed over the houses of the Israelites in Egypt and spared our families when He struck down the Egyptians.'" (Exodus 12:24-28)

YHWH made it clear that this service was to be celebrated by Israelites and their descendants forever. He even told us what to tell our children when asked why we keep the Passover. We remember what He did for our forefathers who were in literal Egypt, and we remember how He delivered the rest of us out of spiritual Egypt (sin).

"Because YHWH kept vigil that night to bring them out of Egypt, on this night all the Israelites are to keep vigil to honor

YHWH for the generations to come. YHWH said to Moses and Aaron, 'These are the regulations for the Passover; No foreigner is to eat of it. Any slave you have bought may eat of it after he is circumcised, but a temporary resident and a hired worker may not eat of it. It must be eaten inside one house, take none of it outside the house. Do not break any of the bones. the whole community of Israel is to celebrate it. An alien living among you who wants to celebrate YHWH's Passover must have all the males in his household circumcised; then he may take part like one native born. no uncircumcised male may eat of it. The same law applies to the native born and to the alien living among you.' " (Exodus 12:42-49)

YHWH then instructed Moses on the regulations regarding His Passover every year after the Exodus. The Israelites are to keep vigil that night to honor YHWH. No foreigner is to eat of it. A foreigner was someone who happened to be in the land, but was not part of Israel and the covenants given to Israel. There were often foreign merchants, traders, and travelers in the land of Israel since Israel contained major trade routes and highways. These people were not to take part in the Passover.

Those who had purchased slaves were to have their slaves circumcised before the slaves were allowed to take part in the family's observance of Passover. Slaves in the Hebrew culture were considered part of the family and would participate in family gatherings and celebrations. They could only participate in the Passover after they were circumcised. Circumcision is the outward sign of being a part of Israel and the covenants that were given to Israel. Yet, YHWH makes it clear throughout scripture that this circumcision must take place in the heart, first. One must desire to be a part of YHWH's people and covenants

(Deuteronomy 10:12-16; 30:6; Jeremiah 4:4; 9:25; Romans 2:25-29).

Aliens were and are non-native born Israelites who desire to become part of YHWH's special people and covenants. They were and are people who come from gentiles who decide to follow and obey YHWH. They were and are grafted into Israel. Their desire to be a part of Israel and the covenants leads to circumcision, first of the heart and then of the flesh. This allows the alien to become like the native-born Israelite and participate in YHWH's Passover.

The Passover meal is to be eaten inside the home, not a church building or community gathering. It is a family meal. Now, if the family is too small for one male lamb or goat, the family is to invite their nearest neighbor (a fellow believer) to join them in order to keep from wasting the meat. None of the meat is to be left over or taken out of the house. Whatever might be left over the next morning is to be burned.

"These are YHWH's appointed feasts, the sacred assemblies you are to proclaim at their appointed times. YHWH's Passover begins at twilight on the fourteenth day of the first month. " (Leviticus 23:4-5)

YHWH had already given the majority of His instructions regarding the Passover meal. In Leviticus He reminded them that it is to take place on the fourteenth day of the first month. This is a full moon either in late March or April. The word "twilight" in the Hebrew text is actually, "between the evenings". Each day began and ended at evening. So, the 14th day of the month began at the evening of the 13th day and lasted until the evening of the 14th when the 15th day began. The term "between the evenings" simply meant at some point between the beginning and ending of the 14th day. It was in that time frame that the lamb or goat was to be slaughtered for the Passover meal. It was then to be cooked and made ready for the family's evening meal.

YHWH spoke to Moses in the desert in the first month of the second year after they came out of Egypt. He said, "Have the Israelites celebrate the Passover at the appointed time. Celebrate it at the appointed time, at twilight on the fourteenth day of this month, in accordance with all its rules and regulations." So, Moses told the Israelites to celebrate the Passover, and they did so in the desert at twilight on the fourteenth day of the first month. The Israelites did everything just as YHWH commanded Moses.

But some of them could not celebrate the Passover on that day because they were ceremonially unclean on account of a dead body. So, they came to Moses and Aaron that same day and said to Moses, "We have become unclean because of a dead body, but why should we be kept from presenting YHWH's offering with the other Israelites at the appointed time?" Moses answered them, "Wait until I find out what YHWH commands concerning you."

Then YHWH told Moses, "Tell the Israelites: 'When any of you or your descendants are unclean because of a dead body or are away on a journey, they may still celebrate YHWH's Passover, but they are to celebrate it on the fourteenth day of the second month at twilight. They are to eat the lamb, together with unleavened bread and bitter herbs. They must not leave any of it until morning or break any of its bones. When they celebrate the Passover, they must follow all the regulations. But if a man who is ceremonially clean and not on a journey fails to celebrate the

Passover, that person is to be cut off from his people because he did not present YHWH's offering at the appointed time. That man will bear the consequences of his sin." (Numbers 9:1-13)

This set of instructions deal with someone who is unable to celebrate YHWH's Passover due to being unclean or on a trip far from home. There were various things that would make a person unclean: contact with a dead body, sexual relations, menstrual cycle, and giving birth. These had nothing to do with sin, but with becoming unclean. An unclean person was not allowed to enter the Tabernacle or Temple until they had been cleansed with water and returned to a state of cleanness. This had more to do with keeping the worship of YHWH separate and distinct from the worship of pagan gods and very little to do with sin.

The people had to be clean to approach the tabernacle and temple with their offering to YHWH. The Passover lambs were slaughtered at the tabernacle or temple. YHWH stated that if one were unclean due to a dead body, or had been traveling and unable to participate in YHWH's Passover, that person could participate in the Passover meal exactly one month later. This is the only feast/service that YHWH allows for another time should one be unable to celebrate at the appointed time.

"Observe the month of Abib and celebrate the Passover of YHWH your Elohim, because in the month of Abib He brought you out of Egypt by night. Sacrifice as the Passover to YHWH your Elohim an animal from your flock or herd at the place YHWH will choose as a dwelling for His Name. Do not eat it with bread made with yeast, but for seven days eat unleavened bread, the bread of affliction, because you left Egypt in haste- so that all the days of your life you may remember the time of your departure from Egypt. Let no yeast be found in your possession in all your land for seven days. Do not let any of the meat you sacrifice on the evening of the first day remain until morning. You must not sacrifice the Passover in any town YHWH your Elohim gives you except in the place He will choose as a dwelling for His Name. There you must sacrifice the Passover in the evening when the, when the sun is going down, on the anniversary of your departure from Egypt. Roast it and eat it at the place YHWH your Elohim will choose." (Deuteronomy 16:1-8)

These are the final instructions given to YHWH's people regarding the Passover. YHWH reminded them to keep the Passover in the first month of the year. He told them very clearly that they were not to sacrifice their animals anywhere except at the tabernacle or temple. Eat the meal with unleavened bread to commemorate the fact that they left Egypt in haste. They were to get rid of all leavened bread and all yeast for the seven days immediately following the Passover meal.

So, what does all this mean to non-native Israelites today? YHWH says that His laws are for the native born and for the non-native born who attach themselves to His people. He had planned, from the beginning, for people from the nations to learn about Him and choose to join Israel. It was His desire that Israel be such a light that many from the nations would choose to worship Him as the one true God (Deuteronomy 4:5-8). Paul made it clear that those of us who follow YHWH through His son Yeshua are grafted into Israel. We do not remain gentiles, nor do we remain apart from Israel. Through Yeshua we are allowed to become citizens of Israel and partakers of the covenants given to Israel (Romans 11:11-24; Ephesians 2:11-22).

PROCLAIM MY FEASTS

If we are part of Israel, we are to be participating in the yearly Feasts that YHWH declared were His. This begins with Passover. We, as believers, are to participate in the Passover meal each year, just as instructed by YHWH. We are to yearly celebrate the salvation that was given us through the blood of the lamb/Lamb of God. Without a temple there are some things that we cannot do, but we are to do the things we can.

For those who do not keep herds:

1. You must be a member of Israel and the covenants
2. You must be circumcised, first of the heart, then of the flesh
3. Eat a meal of lamb, bitter herbs, unleavened bread; whatever else you choose to serve is up to you, as long as it does not contain yeast
4. This is the evening meal on the fourteenth day of the first month of the year
5. Eat all the meat before sunrise, anything left must be burned
6. Eat it in a home with family and/or close neighbors
7. Keep vigil all night to honor YHWH

For those of you who do keep herds:

1. Must be a member of Israel and the covenants
2. Males must be circumcised, first of the heart, then of the flesh
3. On the 10th day of the month you are to choose your lamb or goat
4. Slaughter it on the 14th day of the month, it is not a

sacrifice
5. Prepare the lamb over a fire
6. Meal of lamb, bitter herbs, unleavened bread; whatever else you choose to serve is up to you, as long as it does not contain yeast.
7. Eat meal with family and/or close neighbor (fellow believer) that evening
8. Eat all meat before sunrise, anything left must be burned
9. Keep vigil all night to honor YHWH

There are many, many traditions surrounding the Passover meal. Our first Passover meal was hosted by a Messianic couple and it took two hours to go through all the traditional rituals. Needless to say, my family and I were starving by the time we finally got to the meal! If you want to use some of the traditions that are out there, that is up to you, but remember that they are only traditions, not instructions from YHWH. Don't elevate them to the status of His commands, and don't look down on others who may not do the same things in their celebrations.

Passover is the yearly celebration of our release from bondage in Egypt, physically and spiritually. Passover is also when the Lamb of YHWH was killed. His blood covers those who submit to Him and offers us salvation. Remembering that Passover is to be a reminder of what YHWH did for Israel in Egypt, let's see how this feast also pointed to Yeshua, our Messiah.

1. The Hebrews were in bondage in Egypt.
2. On the 10th day of the month the Israelites were to choose a lamb or goat without blemish.

3. On the 14th day of the month, the lamb was to be slaughtered.
4. The blood of the lamb or goat was put on the doorposts and of the house to cover the first-born who lived there and save them from death.

At the time of Yeshua:

1. On the 10th day of the month the high priest would go to the sheepfolds of Bethlehem and pick out the spotless lamb.
2. The high priest would put the lamb on the back of a donkey or carry it in order to keep it from blemish.
3. The lamb would be staked in the courtyard of the temple for four days where everyone was welcome to inspect the lamb for blemish; making sure that the lamb really was spotless. The lamb would be slaughtered along with the evening sacrifice.
4. We are in bondage to sin
5. Yeshua was born in Bethlehem where the shepherds were told that the Lamb of YHWH was born.
6. The year that he was crucified he entered Jerusalem on the back of a donkey on the tenth day of the month as the Lamb of God and the High Priest of God.
7. He then spent three days in the courtyards of the temple teaching and being questioned.
8. On the fourth day of inspection, or 14th day of the month, he was before the Sanhedrin and before Pilate. None could find blemish in him.
9. He was then crucified and died about the time of the

evening sacrifice.
10. He was taken off the cross before sunset so that nothing of the Passover lamb remained till sunrise.
11. His blood covers those who submit to him and saves us from eternal death.

Some believe that the last supper he was having with his disciples was the Passover meal. Some will claim that he and his disciples ate the Passover meal on the evening of the thirteenth day and he was crucified on the fourteenth day. Some claim that he ate it on the fourteenth day but that the rest of Israel was celebrating the meal on the fifteenth. I find it very hard to accept either of these claims.

If Yeshua ate the Passover meal on the thirteenth, then he was not obeying YHWH's commands to eat it on the fourteenth. He would be sinning and would therefore not be the spotless Lamb. If he ate it on the fourteenth while the rest of Israel ate it on the fifteenth, then he was not the Passover Lamb. The Passover lamb had to be slaughtered on the fourteenth of the month. The only way Yeshua could have been the spotless Passover Lamb was if he obeyed everything that YHWH instructed and was killed on the fourteenth of the month. This leaves the claim that his last supper was the Passover meal without much merit.

There are several more reasons that I do not believe that our Savior was eating the Passover meal.

1. There is absolutely no mention of a lamb, bitter herbs, or unleavened bread
2. The disciples believed that Judas was going to go

purchase something for the feast. If they were eating the Passover meal, it was the beginning of a special Sabbath. Nothing would be open for making purchases. Why would they believe he was going to purchase something for the feast if it was the beginning of a special Sabbath? And if they were eating the feast, why would they think he needed to go purchase something more?

3. The Jewish leaders wanted Yeshua killed before the feast. They did not want him on the cross during the feast, nor have him on trial during the feast. They wanted all the unpleasantness of killing Yeshua done with before the Passover meal.
4. The Jewish leaders presented Yeshua to Pilate but would not enter Pilate's buildings in order to keep from becoming traditionally unclean. They knew they needed to be clean in order to offer their sacrifices and have their lamb slaughtered at the temple.
5. The Jews wanted the bodies taken off of the crosses before sunset because the next day was a special Sabbath, the first day of Unleavened Bread. The first day of Unleavened Bread is on the fifteenth of the month. Wanting the bodies off the crosses and buried before the special Sabbath shows that Israel was not eating the Passover meal on the evening of the fifteenth day of the month.

Those are just a few of the reasons that I personally hold to the belief that the last supper was not the Passover meal. However, you can see that the Passover and its rituals as instructed by YHWH pointed to Yeshua our Messiah. Today, the meal is still YHWH's Passover. He passed over those who were covered with the blood of the lamb in Egypt and spared them from death. Those covered by the blood of Yeshua are spared from eternal spiritual death.

Who would not want to celebrate these two examples of salvation from our God each year?! It is a glorious thing that we who are grafted into Israel are allowed to join in on the celebration of YHWH's Passover. I hope that you and your family will enjoy celebrating this feast together in honor of our God and Savior. May your time with Him be blessed!

ג

Chapter 3

Unleavened Bread
Connected to YHWH's Passover is the Feast of Unleavened Bread. This feast is exactly what its name signifies, a celebration with bread that is not leavened. The first instructions for this feast are also in Exodus 12.

" For seven days you are to eat bread made without yeast. On the first day remove the yeast from your houses for whoever eats anything with yeast in it from the first day through the seventh day must be cut off from Israel. On the first day hold a sacred assembly and another one on the seventh day. Do no work at all on these days, except to prepare food for everyone to eat- that is all you may do.

Celebrate the Feast of Unleavened Bread because it was on this day that I brought your divisions out of Egypt. Celebrate this day as a lasting ordinance for the generations to come. IN the first month you are to eat bread made without yeast, from the evening of the fourteenth day until the evening of the twenty-first day. For seven days no yeast is to be found in your houses. And whoever eats anything with yeast in it must be cut off from the community of Israel, whether he is an alien or native born. Eat nothing with yeast. Wherever you live you must eat unleavened bread." (Exodus 12:15-20)

Beginning with the Passover meal, YHWH's people are to go seven days without leavened bread. The Hebrew word that is translated as leavening or yeast is "seor". The Hebrews did not have yeast packets nor were they able to go to the store and purchase yeast, baking soda, or baking powder. They would mix up a starter with flour and water which would be left to sit on a counter or table. This starter would collect yeast from the air. After a few days this seor could be used. The woman would pull a piece from the seor and set it aside to continue collecting yeast. The bulk of the seor would be added to her ingredients, kneaded into the dough, and allowed to rise. The seor is what would make the bread rise.

YHWH was specifically speaking to the seor that was used to make bread rise. On the fifteenth day of the first month all Israel is to get rid of all seor and all bread made with it. Beginning with the Passover meal eaten on the prior evening Israel is to be without leavened bread or leavening (seor) for seven full days.

"For seven days eat bread made without yeast and on the seventh day hold a festival to YHWH. Eat unleavened bread during those seven days; nothing with yeast is to be seen among you, nor shall any yeast be seen anywhere within your borders. On that day tell your son, 'I do this because of what YHWH did for me when I came out of Egypt.' This observance will be for you like a sign on your hand and a reminder on your forehead that the law of YHWH is to be on your lips. For YHWH brought you out of Egypt with His mighty hand. You must keep this ordinance at the appointed time year after year." (Exodus 13:6-10)

The rest of chapter 13 spells out more details about the first day of Unleavened Bread, including a special sabbath on the first and seventh days of the week, the redemption of the first-born sons, and the sacrifice of every firstborn male of their livestock. These regulations were to impress upon YHWH's people the gravity of their redemption from Egypt and the value that YHWH places upon the firstborn sons. He told us that Israel is

His firstborn and He redeemed Israel. His people were to do the same with their first-born sons. However, the current lack of a temple and Aaronic priesthood would prevent us from carrying out these instructions at this time.

"Three times a year you are to celebrate a Festival to me. Celebrate the Feast of Unleavened Bread for seven days eat bread made without yeast, as I commanded you. Do this at the appointed time in the month of Abib, for in that month you came out of Egypt." (Exodus 23:14-15)

Unleavened Bread is one of the three major feasts for which YHWH expected His people to travel to the tabernacle or temple to bring Him special offerings. Each man would bring an offering of his choosing, the redemption price for his firstborn son, and offer up the firstborn males of the livestock. This was done on the fifteenth day of the first month to commemorate the anniversary of the day YHWH took them out of Egypt.

"These are YHWH's appointed feasts, the sacred assemblies you are to proclaim at their appointed times; YHWH's Passover begins at twilight on the fourteenth day of the first month. On the fifteenth day of that month YHWH's Feast of Unleavened Bread begins; for seven days you must eat bread made without yeast. On the first day hold a sacred assembly and do no regular work. For seven days present an offering made to YHWH by fire. And on the seventh day hold a sacred assembly and do no regular work." (Leviticus 23:4-8.)

In addition to eating unleavened bread for seven days and redeeming the firstborn of every womb, YHWH also instructed that the first and seventh days of the week of Unleavened Bread should be sacred assemblies of His people. These two days are to be special sabbaths similar to the regular weekly Sabbath. This is also the first place that YHWH mentions the priests are to offer up special sacrifices in addition to the regular daily sacrifices.

"Observe the month of Abib and celebrate the Passover of YHWH your Elohim, because in the month of Abib He brought you out of Egypt by night. Sacrifice as the Passover to YHWH your Elohim an animal from your flock or heard at the place YHWH will choose as a dwelling for His Name. Do not eat it with bread made with yeast, but for seven days eat unleavened bread, the bread of affliction, because you left Egypt in haste-so that all the days of your life you may remember the time of your departure from Egypt. Let no yeast be found in your possession in all your land for seven days." (Deuteronomy 16:1-4).

Again, we are told to celebrate the Feast of Unleavened Bread, beginning with the Passover meal, for seven days. For seven days there is not to be any yeast (seor) in the house nor are we to eat any bread leavened with yeast. It is to remind us of the haste in which YHWH took us out of Egypt, physically and spiritually.

So, how does this point to Yeshua? Remember that on this day, the fifteenth of the first month, all the firstborn sons were to be redeemed. A sacrifice had to be offered in place of the firstborn son, and all firstborn of the livestock were to be sacrificed. This was a reminder that YHWH had taken the lives of the Egyptians for the lives of Israel, YHWH's firstborn son.

After Yeshua died on the cross, Joseph and Nicodemus took down his body, anointed him with oils, and wrapped his body. They then put his body in a tomb. The Lamb of YHWH had been offered up in place of Israel to spiritually redeem His people. He died that we might live. The Lamb was lying in the tomb on the fifteenth day of the month, paying the redemption price for us. Because of him we were able to leave the bondage of Egypt (sin) in haste. It was immediate and it was affected by YHWH Himself. He was given in place of, in redemption of the first born, Israel.

Yeshua was placed in the tomb just before sunset of the fourteenth day of the month in order that the disciples might be able to bury him before the first day of Unleavened Bread began. At sunset, it became the fifteenth day of the month, the first day of Unleavened Bread and a special sabbath. The scriptures tell us that the disciples rested on that day as commanded.

"Now there was a man named Joseph, a member of the council, a good and upright man, who had not consented to their decision and action. He came from the Judean town of Arimathea and he was waiting for the kingdom of Elohim. Going to Pilate he asked for Yeshua's body. They he took it down, wrapped it in linen cloth and placed it in a tomb cut in the rock, one in which no one had yet been laid. It was Preparation Day, and the Sabbath was about to begin.

The women who had come with Yeshua from Galilee followed Joseph and saw the tomb and how his body was laid in it. Then they went home and prepared spices and perfumes. But they rested on the Sabbath in obedience to the commandment." (Luke 23:50-56)

"When the Sabbath was over, Mary Magdalene, Mary the mother of James, and Salome bought spices so that they might go to anoint Yeshua's body." (Mark 16:1)

These verses sound as if they are contradicting each other. Luke says that the women prepared the spices before resting on the Sabbath, and Mark records that after the Sabbath the women bought spices. Are they contradictory? Of course not. If they were, the Bible would not be the true Word of God. When you realize that Unleavened Bread is a special sabbath in addition to the weekly Sabbath, they make perfect sense. Luke is recording the day before the first day of Unleavened Bread which is a special sabbath. Mark mentions the weekly Sabbath.

That specific year Wednesday was Preparation Day, the day everyone prepared their Passover Meal. It was the day our Messiah was crucified. Thursday was the first day of Unleavened Bread. Friday was the day the women went to purchase the spices and prepare them. Saturday was the weekly Sabbath. Sunday the women went to the tomb to find it already empty.

So, how do we celebrate this feast today? There is no temple or proper priesthood, so we do not go to the temple to redeem our firstborn sons. However, we are to take yeast and bread with yeast in it out of our houses. Throw it away. Eat unleavened bread for seven days.

Yeshua made it clear that yeast represents false doctrines, false beliefs, false humility, and false religions. In Matthew 16:5-12 he warned us to avoid the yeast of the Pharisees (religious leaders). Paul also indicated that sin or associating with sin is also symbolized by yeast (1Corinthians 5:1-8). This time of year is a very good time to evaluate your doctrines, beliefs, and other things in your life and home. If any of them are false- if they are contrary to YHWH's word- they need to be eliminated for good. Those things, along with the bread and yeast you have, must be taken out of the house and eliminated.

To summarize, this is the list of commands concerning Unleavened Bread:

1. Rest on first and seventh day of Unleavened Bread,

preparation of a meal allowed
2. Eliminate yeast and leavened bread from your home
3. Meet with YHWH and His people on the first and seventh day
4. Rejoice in our redemption

There are many traditions and man-made rules that have evolved around this feast; mainly that a person is to eliminate anything that might "puff up". This includes baking soda, baking powder, rice, beans, etc... There are those who even get rid of their dog or cat food if it has yeast. Some even throw out brewer's yeast and nutritional yeast which have nothing to do with baking bread. If it is your desire to do this, then by all means do it for YHWH. But, it is not commanded and therefore is not to be expected of those who celebrate His feasts.

Remember Yeshua told us that his yoke is easy, his burden is light. His instructions to us concerning the feasts are also easy and light. They are a joy and a celebration!

ד

Chapter 4

First Fruits

In the midst of the week of Unleavened Bread there is another holy day that we are to celebrate, the Feast of First Fruits. First Fruits does not have as many instructions concerning it, but that does not make it any less of a holy day in YHWH's calendar. It is still one of His holy days and He asks us to celebrate it.

Then YHWH said to Moses, "Speak to the Israelites and say to them, 'When you enter the land I am going to give you and you reap its harvest, bring to the priest a sheaf of the first grain you harvest. he is to wave the sheaf before YHWH so it will be accepted on your behalf; the priest is to wave it on the day after the Sabbath. On the day you wave the Sheaf, you must sacrifice as a burnt offering to YHWH a lamb a year old without defect, together with its grain offering of two tenths of an ephah of fine flour mixed with oil- an offering made to YHWH by fire, a pleasing aroma- and its drink offering of a quarter of a hin of wine. You must not eat any bread, or roasted or new grain, until the very day you bring this offering to your Elohim. This is to be a lasting ordinance for the generations to come, wherever you live.'" (Leviticus 23:9-14)

This is the only place we find any instructions for the feast known as First Fruits. This day is always on a Sunday according to the names we use on our calendar. It occurs the Sunday after Passover. The people were each to cut the first sheaf of the barley crop, bring it to the temple, and present it to the priest. The priest was to wave before the altar each sheaf offered. Each sheaf would then go into the storage areas to be used by the priests for their own flour and bread. The priests were also commanded to offer up a special sacrifice on this day in addition to the regular daily sacrifices.

YHWH declared that there was not to be any harvesting of the rest of the barley crop until this sheaf had been waved before the altar. Since the people depended upon their crops to live, it was very important that this offering be made when instructed so the harvest could commence.

As with the other holy days, First Fruits points us to Yeshua. How? First Fruits was the day upon which Yeshua was resurrected from the dead! All four gospels record for us that the tomb was found empty very early on the first day of the week (Sunday). John added another element to the resurrection. In chapter 20, John recorded that Mary saw Yeshua and ran toward him. Yeshua told her "Do not hold on to me, for I have not yet returned to the Father. Go instead to my brothers and tell them, 'I am returning to my Father and your Father, to my Elohim and your Elohim.' " (John 20:17)

Why did Yeshua mention this? He had been resurrected for several hours by the time anyone came to the tomb, yet, he still had not returned to YHWH. He had not appeared before the throne of our God even though he had been dead. His soul (human) had laid in rest and the spirit that comes from God to give mankind life had returned to fill the body and soul with life once more. Yet, he still needed to appear before the throne of YHWH as the wave offering- the first fruits of the dead.

Just as the barley harvest could not occur until the first sheaf was waved before the altar, the resurrection of the dead to eternal life could not occur until the resurrected Messiah had appeared before the throne of YHWH, his Father. His resurrection as the first fruits of the dead opened up the way for the future resurrection that will take place on his second coming. At that time, those who died in him will be raised to eternal life with him.

"But Messiah has indeed been raised from the dead, the first fruits of those who have fallen asleep. For since death came through a man, the resurrection of the dead comes also through a man. For as in Adam all die, so in Messiah all will be made alive. but each in his own turn; Messiah the first fruits; then, when he comes, those who belong to him. " (1 Corinthians 15:1-26)

This holy day is the first day of the barley harvest in the agricultural world that opens the door to the greater harvest. It is the day of our Messiah's resurrection that opens the door for the resurrection of our souls from the dead. How do we celebrate this feast?

Well, first of all, we do not celebrate it on the day called Easter. We do not celebrate with bunnies, eggs, chocolate, or sunrise services. It is to be on the Sunday following the Passover meal. It is to be remembered as the actual day our Messiah rose from the dead! It is to be celebrated because we will one day be resurrected from the dead to eternal life.

It is also considered day one of counting the omer which is commanded in Leviticus 23:15-21. From the day of First Fruits we are to count seven full weeks and hold a celebration on the fiftieth day. That celebration is Shavuot.

1. Meet with YHWH and His people
2. A day of rest- special Sabbath
3. Rejoice in the resurrection of our Master and Savior
4. Celebrate the future resurrection to eternal life for all

who live in Yeshua
5. begin counting the days till the Feast of Shavuot

Any traditions you may add must avoid any appearance of being related to Easter, the pagan holiday that celebrates the return of the fertility goddess from the underworld. It is most unfortunate that the Catholic Church chose to attach the amazing miracle of our Messiah's resurrection to the day of fertility worship. Praise YHWH we can return to His holy day and celebrate His work on the actual day He performed that work!

Chapter 5

Shavuot

The fourth feast in YHWH's calendar of holy days is Shavuot. That is the Hebrew name for what is called the Feast of Weeks. This feast takes place 50 days after First Fruits. I admit that our family did not really make much of this feast in the first several years that we celebrated YHWH's holy days. We acknowledged it, but not much more than that.

Then, one year as we were preparing for Passover, YHWH spoke to me. He reminded me that when we celebrated the holiday of Christmas, we looked forward to that day with a great anticipation. We counted the days till Christmas and could not wait for it to arrive. He specifically planted the Feast of Shavuot in my mind and asked me, "Why do you not anticipate my holy days like you used to anticipate those holidays of man?"

My heart was pierced! My King was right. I had tended to skip over the "lesser" feasts, especially since there was so much that could not be done without a temple or proper priest hood. That year I took to heart what YHWH had asked me and poured myself into purposely looking forward to His feasts. That included a counting of the days between First Fruits and Shavuot, and working to prepare a city-wide celebration of Shavuot.

That celebration was amazing for me! I learned how to truly celebrate Shavuot. As a large group we followed His instructions for the feast. Ever since that year, there is not a single feast that I feel is "lesser" or not as important. I realized that to YHWH they are all important because they are His holy days.

" From the day after the Sabbath, the day you brought the sheaf of the wave offering, count off seven full weeks. Count off fifty days up to the day after the seventh Sabbath, and then present an offering of new grain to YHWH. From wherever you live, bring two loaves made of two tenths of an ephah of fine flour, bake with yeast, as a wave offering of first fruits to YHWH. Present with this bread seven male lambs, each a year old and without defect, one young bull and two rams. They will be a burnt offering made by fire, and aroma pleasing to YHWH. Then sacrifice one male goat for a purification offering and two lambs, each a year old for a fellowship offering. The priest is to wave the two lambs before YHWH as a wave offering, together with the bread of the first fruits. They are a sacred offering to YHWH for the priest. On that same day you are to proclaim a sacred assembly and do no regular work. This is to be a lasting ordinance for the generations to come, wherever you live. " (Leviticus 23:15-21)

"Three times a year you are to celebrate a festival to me...No one is to appear before me empty handed. Celebrate the Feast of Harvest with the first fruits of the crops you sow in your fields." (Exodus 23:14-18)

The Hebrews call the fourth holy day on YHWH's calendar Shavuot. Scripture also calls it, in the English language, Feast of Harvest and Feast of Weeks. The Hebrews also called it Second First Fruits. It takes place fifty days after First Fruits and the people were instructed to travel to the tabernacle or temple. They were to bring the first fruits of every other crop, besides barley, to the priest. This would include the very first of the fruit and nut trees, wheat, and everything else that would be growing at that time.

The Hebrews called the counting of these 50 days "counting the omer". An omer was a unit of measurement similar to our unit of measurement we call a liter. It was used to measure amounts of wheat, flour, or any other dry ingredient used in every day baking or cooking.

"Count off seven weeks from the time you begin to put the sickle to the standing grain. Then celebrate the Feast of Weeks to YHWH your Elohim by giving a freewill offering in proportion to the blessings YHWH your Elohim has given you. And rejoice before YHWH your Elohim at the place He will choose as a dwelling for His Name- you, your sons and daughters, your menservants and maidservants, the Levites in your towns, and the aliens, the fatherless and the widows living among you. Remember that you were slaves in Egypt and follow carefully these decrees." (Deuteronomy 16:9-12)

Again, we were instructed to count off seven full weeks, then on the fiftieth day hold a celebration to YHWH at the place He chose. We were to bring a freewill offering consisting of the first fruits of our crops along with two loaves of bread baked with yeast. This counting begins on the day of First Fruits and goes for seven full weeks with the Feast of Shavuot taking place on the fiftieth day which will always be a Sunday on the secular calendar.

"When you have entered the land YHWH your Elohim is giving you as an inheritance and have taken possession of it and settled in it, take some of the first fruits of all that you produce from the soil of the land YHWH your Elohim is giving you and put them in a basket. Then go to the place YHWH your Elohim will choose as a dwelling for His Name and say to the priest in office at the time, 'I declare today to YHWH your Elohim that I have come to the land YHWH swore to our forefathers to give us' The priest shall take the basket from your hands and set it down in front of the altar of YHWH your Elohim. Then you shall declare before YHWH your Elohim, 'My father was a wandering Aramean, and he went down into Egypt with a few people and lived there and became a great nation, powerful and numerous. But the Egyptians mistreated us and made us suffer, putting us to hard labor. Then we cried out to YHWH the Elohim of our fathers and YHWH hear our voice and saw our misery, toil, and oppression. So, YHWH brought us out of Egypt with a mighty hand and an outstretched arm, with great terror and with miraculous signs and wonders. He brought us to this place and gave us this land, and land flowing with milk and honey; and now I bring the firstfruits of the soil that you O YHWH have given me.' place the basket before YHWH you Elohim and bow down before Him. And you and the Levites and the aliens among you shall rejoice in all the good things YHWH your Elohim has given you and your household." (Deuteronomy 26:1-11)

This section of scripture gave the people more instruction on what specifically they were to do on the Feast of Shavuot. They were to put their first fruits into a basket and take it to the priest. The priest would set it before the altar of YHWH and the person presenting it would recite the history of YHWH's people. This feast was a reminder of all YHWH had done for them from the very beginning right up to the point they were presenting their offerings.

1. Count fifty days from the day of First Fruits
2. Go to the tabernacle or temple with first fruits of all crops

3. Present first fruits in basket to priest who set it before the altar
4. Recite the history of YHWH's people and remember all He has done

As per all the feasts, this one also points us to Yeshua. After the resurrection of Yeshua, he spent forty of the fifty days till Shavuot teaching his disciples and proving that he was the Messiah. He was giving them understanding into the scriptures that spoke about him. He was preparing them for life without his physical presence on this earth. He also promised them a gift, the Holy Spirit, his spirit within us.

On the day of Shavuot, the disciples were at the temple celebrating the feast as instructed. They would have given their gifts and offerings while reciting their history and the blessings of YHWH as instructed. However, that particular Shavuot, they received the gift Yeshua had promised, the Holy Spirit! Due to that gift the apostles were able to convey in other languages the history of YHWH's people and the blessings of YHWH, including the risen Messiah. (Acts 2)

How are we supposed to celebrate today?

1. Count off fifty days beginning with First Fruits as day one
2. Rest and do not work, a special sabbath
3. Recite the history of YHWH's people (us)

(remember)

1. Count our blessings as individuals and as His people

2. Celebrate the fact we have the Holy Spirit within us and use the gifts it gives us to edify the Body

(rehearse)

1. Present a freewill offering to YHWH to be used for the needy and for those who are specifically doing Kingdom work.

That first year that we truly celebrated this feast I had planned for some speakers to teach on the Holy Spirit. After all, Shavuot is the day it was poured out upon all YHWH's believers. However, the Spirit made it very clear to me that we were to follow YHWH's instructions about reciting our history.

We spent the day with nearly every member in our congregation taking turns reading from scripture our history from Genesis through the apostolic writings, or praying prayers of repentance as His people. But we did not stop there, because we know that we have an amazing future! We also read scriptures that tell of that future kingdom and His people dwelling with Yeshua. It truly did change my thinking about this particular feast.

Anything else is up to you. Just know that we, as YHWH's people, have a much longer history to recite now than the generation who entered the promised land. We, as His people, have many more blessings to count and for which to give thanks. Simply reciting can be boring, but this is to be a celebration! So, find ways to anticipate this day and make this an amazing celebration for the whole congregation.

As people who have been grafted in to Israel, we are part of Israel. Therefore, Israel's history is our history. This particular day the men are to recite our history to keep it fresh in the minds of the older generations and to teach the younger generations. I have included the Scriptures that our congregation used that first year so that you may have an overview of the history (and future) of Israel. Just remember that Israel's (our) history did not end when Jerusalem was destroyed in AD 70. There is so much more for our generation to remember in how God has been faithful to His people.

• • • •

GENESIS 12 AND 15
    Exodus 19:1-6, 16-25
    Exodus 20 1-21
    Numbers 13 and 14
    Numbers 23:19-23
    Numbers 24:5-9
    Nehemiah 1:5-11
    Deuteronomy 30:11-20
    Deuteronomy 32:1-43
    1 Chronicles 16:8-36
    1 Chronicles 29:10-13
    Nehemiah 9:5-31; 13:31
    Psalm 8
    Psalm 19
    Psalm 24
    Psalm 78
    Psalm 25
    Psalm 91

Psalm 92
Psalm 96
Psalm 119:169-176
Isaiah 11
Daniel 9:4-19
Jeremiah 16:14-21
Jeremiah 23:1-8
Jeremiah 31:1-4
Ezekiel 11:16-21
Psalm 51
Ezekiel 20:33-38
Ezekiel 34:11-16
Ezekiel 36:22-28
Ezekiel 37:15-28
Micah 7:18-20
Amos 9:11-15
Micah 4:1-8
Luke 1:46-55, 68-75
Matthew 26:30-68
Matthew 27:32- Matthew 28:20
Acts 2
Psalm 103
Revelation 4:8,11
Revelation 5:9-13
Revelation 7:10-12
Revelation 11:17-18
Revelation 15:3-4
Revelation 19:5-9
Revelation 20
Revelation 21

PROCLAIM MY FEASTS

Revelation 22
Psalm 119:33-37
Psalm 106:47-48

ו

Chapter 6

Feast of Trumpets

The fifth feast in YHWH's cycle of holy days is the Feast of Trumpets. The Hebrew word translated as trumpets in this feast is "teruah". It means "clamor, acclamation of joy or a battle cry; clangor of trumpets as an alarm; splitting of the ears". The instructions for this feast are very few and simple.

YHWH said to Moses, "Say to the Israelites, 'On the first day of the seventh month you are to have a day of rest, a sacred assembly commemorated with trumpet blasts. Do no regular work, but present an offering made to YHWH by fire.' " (Leviticus 23:23-25)

"On the first day of the seventh month hold a sacred assembly and do no regular work. It is a day for you to sound the trumpets." (Numbers 29:1-2)

They were to set aside the first day of the seventh month for a memorial, signaled or commemorated with "clamor, acclamation of joy or a battle cry; clangor of trumpets as an alarm; splitting of the ears". However, there is nothing to indicate what is being remembered. YHWH simply tell us to have a day of rest and a sacred assembly. Of course, while there was a tabernacle or temple, the priests offered a special sacrifice along with the regular daily sacrifices.

This day was celebrated in the local towns. This was not a feast for which the families were to travel to the tabernacle or temple to meet with YHWH. They met with Him in their hometowns.

What would we be remembering that would be signaled or commemorated with trumpets? Perhaps YHWH expected His people to remember when they heard His voice on the mountain. At that time, they also heard a loud sound like a trumpet (Exodus 19:19; 20:18). Imagine how it must have been to experience a supernatural blowing of a trumpet while hearing the voice of YHWH!

However, remember that these feasts are also a rehearsal. In the prophets we are told a great deal about times that will be accompanied by a trumpet sound. These prophecies tell us that many of the events of the end days will be accompanied by the sound of a trumpet (Isaiah 27:12-12; Isaiah 58:1; Ezekiel 33:3; Zephaniah 1:14-18; Matthew 24:31; Revelation 8:13). The prophets and apostles also tell us that in the future we will all hear a trumpet at the return of our Messiah (Zechariah 9:14-17; 1 Corinthians 15:52; 1 Thessalonians 4:16). The apostle John describes the voice of Yeshua whom he saw while on the isle of Patmos as being like a loud trumpet sound (Revelation 1:10; 4:1). These are all things to ponder as we celebrate this feast on the first day of the seventh month.

Now this feast is also considered the one "no man knows the day or hour". It is on the first of the seventh month. This is usually late September or October on our secular calendars. The Hebrew calendar is determined by the moon. The first of the month is determined by the sighting of the new moon. Usually the day after the new moon is day one of the month. One had to be watching the phases of the moon each month to determine the first day of the month. Only as one got closer to the new moon of the seventh month would there be any idea of the exact day to celebrate the Feast of Trumpets.

The instructions for celebrating today are the same as back then, minus the sacrifices offered by the priests.

"Say to the Israelites, "On the first day of the seventh month you are to have a day of rest, a sacred assembly commemorated with trumpets. Do no regular work, but present an offering by fire to YHWH." (Leviticus 23:23-25)

1. Rest, do no regular work
2. Meet with YHWH and with His people
3. Make lots of noise, blow trumpets!
4. Remember (His voice on Mt Sinai?) and rehearse (the return of our Messiah!)

As with all the feasts, there are many man-made traditions that have been developed over the years. Just remember that the commands from YHWH are simple and hold weight over any tradition. Otherwise, have a great time making as much noise as you and your congregation can. One day in the near future, our joyful noises will be accompanied by the trumpets that announce the arrival of our King! Hallelu Yah!

Just a note concerning the new moon: there are different ideas as to when the new moon is specifically. Some say it is the very first sliver of the moon that can be seen with the naked eye. Others believe that it is the conjunction of the moon when the sun and moon are together and the moon cannot be seen.

Those who watch for a sliver will watch for it at night, close to sunset. The sliver seen just before sunset signals that day one of the month begins at that sunset. Those who watch for a conjunction will watch for it in the morning close to sunrise. While a slight sliver of the moon is visible the morning before, on the day of the conjunction there is nothing to see in the morning. The sunset that follows begins day one of the month.

Scripture does not tell us which one is the first of the month. In fact, the English words, "new moon" are actually a translation for the Hebrew word "chodesh" which means "new" or "renew" but implies a month. There is a completely different word for "moon." None of the scriptures give specifics on whether the new moon is when it is dark or when it is a sliver. Whichever you choose, remember that only when Yeshua returns will we truly know how to mark a new month.

PROCLAIM MY FEASTS

Chapter 7

Day of Atonements

The sixth feast on YHWH's calendar is Day of Atonements. What is an atonement? The Hebrew word is "kaphar". It is a primitive root meaning "to cover, to expiate or condone, to placate, or cancel, to appease, cleanse, disannul, forgive, pardon, and even reconcile." Atonement is a substitution and covering that allows one to find forgiveness and reconciliation with YHWH. A substitution was made in place of the death of the sinner.

Leviticus 16 give us the very first instructions concerning this particular holy day. It lays out how the High Priest would present atonement for his sins, then approach the mercy seat of YHWH in the Most Holy Place to present atonement for the sins of Israel as a nation. The High Priest would then sacrifice a goat out of a selected pair of wild goats. He would lay his hands on the second goat of the pair, declare all the sins of Israel, and send the goat out into the wilderness never to return. This is all a very interesting process. The whole chapter deals with the High Priest's actions on the Day of Atonements.

Let's look at scripture to find how the people were to celebrate.

YHWH said to Moses, "The tenth day of this seventh month is the Day of Atonements. Hold a sacred assembly and afflict yourselves and present an offering made by fire to YHWH. Do not work on that day, because it is the Day of Atonements, when atonement is made for you before YHWH your Elohim. Anyone who does not afflict himself on that day must be cut off from his people. I will destroy from among his people anyone who does any work on that day. you shall do no work at all. This is to be a lasting ordinance for the generations to come wherever you live. It is a Sabbath of rest for you, and you must afflict yourselves. From the evening of the ninth day of the month until the following evening you are to observe this Sabbath." (Leviticus 23:26-32)

To summarize the instructions given:

1. Do not work, a special sabbath
2. Meet with YHWH and His people- sacred assembly locally
3. Afflict oneself
4. The priest presented an offering by fire to YHWH
5. First for himself, then for the nation of Israel.
6. The priest made atonement for the nation with blood of a goat
7. The live goat is sent into the wilderness bearing the guilt of the nation

On this day the High Priest made atonement for the nation. Atonement was made for the people, not by the people. They did not participate in any part of the activities that took place that day other than to meet with the local assembly. Most people were not even in Jerusalem when these things happened since it was not one of the feasts for which YHWH instructed the people travel to the tabernacle or temple. The things that took place in the tabernacle and later the temple were not even seen by the majority of the nation. They had to trust that the High

Priest was doing what he was instructed to do and was making atonement for the people of the nation.

I believe this is the reason that it is on this feast that YHWH makes the very severe statement that anyone who works on this day is to be cut off from his people. That person is to be kicked out of the camp and will be cut off from Israel both physically and spiritually. That whole day was (and is) about the work of the High Priest. He is the only one to be working on that day. To be working implies that you are rebellious against what Yah has instructed. I believe it also takes away from the importance and righteousness of our High Priest's work in atoning for each person and Israel as a whole.

This feast points to Yeshua as our High Priest who has made atonement for the spiritual nation of Israel in the heavenly tabernacle. He is the perfect High Priest since he will not die and he did not have to make atonement for himself first. He presented his blood at the mercy seat of YHWH on our behalf. All this was unseen by those who are covered (Hebrews 4:14-5:10; 7:1-10:18).

Today the Day of Atonements is a day of mercy. In the future it will be a day of judgment against all who are not covered by the blood of Yeshua. It will be a day of judgment against the nations that do not submit to YHWH. There will come a time when mercy will no longer be found at the throne of our King.

How do we celebrate this feast today?

1. Rest, do not work at all
2. Afflict yourself
3. Meet with YHWH and His people
4. Celebrate the atonement that was made for you

(remember)
5. Prepare for the day of judgment to come upon the nations by getting right with YHWH, confess the sins of the Body (rehearse)

Now, this brings us to the word afflict. What does it mean to afflict oneself? Well, many English versions translate this as "fast". It became tradition to fast on this day. However, fasting is not commanded. The Hebrew word for afflict is "anah". This root word means "to eye, to heed, pay attention, announce, sing or speak, to give an account." From that root word there is also the extension of meaning "to look down, to bow, to humble." From this it is possible to believe that YHWH's people are to pay attention to the day, give an account for oneself, and to humble oneself.

The Jewish rabbis added a great deal of tradition to this day, especially after the destruction of Jerusalem in AD 70. They taught that the day was more about individual judgment than the judgment of the nations. It became more about the individual's sins that needed atonement than the sins of the nation as a whole. They began teaching that YHWH opened His book of life on this day each year and determined who would or would not be written in His book of life for the next year. This led to everyone spending the ten days between Trumpets and Day of Atonements seeking forgiveness from YHWH and from everyone they might have offended during the year.

These traditions take away from the very fact that YHWH said that atonement was made for us. The High Priest has taken care of that atonement. We should seek forgiveness when we have wronged YHWH or another person, but that should be done every day, not once a year. Nor should we see it as a means of ensuring that our names are in the book of life. That is a work of our own in order to attempt to secure spiritual and eternal reconciliation. Seek forgiveness when needed, but leave the atonement work to Yeshua who has already accomplished it in the heavens. Trust that those who believe in him and obey YHWH already have their names in the book of life as is indicated in the Scriptures.

It is obvious in reading the words of the prophets that the Israelites had already made changes to YHWH's feasts and were doing their own things. It did not please YHWH. He specifically spoke to their form of "fasting" on His holy days. The whole chapter of Isaiah 58 deals with what YHWH truly desires on His feasts.

"Is this not the kind of fasting I have chosen; to loose the chains of injustice and untie the cords of the yoke, to set the oppressed free and break every yoke? Is it not to share your food with the hungry and to provide the poor wanderer with shelter- when you see the naked, to clothe him, and not to turn away from your own flesh and blood?"

(verses 6 and 7)

Nowhere in scripture did YHWH instruct us to fast from food and water. He did however ask us to humble ourselves. In Isaiah He gives a good description of what that humbling should look like in our lives. Yeshua repeats this when he taught concerning the day of judgment. He told us that we are to be taking care of the stranger, the sick, the prisoner, and the needy among His people. Whatever we do for His people in love, we do for him (Matthew 25:46).

There are many ways to humble ourselves before YHWH and before our fellow believers. Yeshua said that we are to act as a child and we are to love YHWH with all our hearts, souls, minds, and strength, and love our neighbor as ourselves. These things mean more to YHWH than going 24 hours without food or water.

For those of us in western countries with lots of wealth, fasting from food for a day is definitely an affliction of sorts. It is good practice for learning to live with less and for allowing the body to cleanse itself without the work of digestion for a time. Fasting also has definite spiritual benefits.

If you choose to fast, please be careful. Pregnant women and people with illnesses, such as diabetes, need to take care of themselves and not purposely put themselves in danger. Children will need some nourishment during the day, so it might be possible to fast from solid foods and spend a day only drinking fruit and veggie smoothies. Be patient with children and with yourself. For someone who has never skipped a meal, fasting 24 hours can be a challenge.

Whatever else you and your family and your congregation choose to do, be sure that your motivation is always to honor YHWH according to what He has instructed. Rest in the work that Yeshua has done for you. Enjoy and celebrate this day of mercy and atonements!

Chapter 8

Feast of Tabernacles
  The last feast in the calendar of our King is the Feast of Tabernacles, called Sukkot in Hebrew. This is the climax of the feasts! It was the last feast of the cycle and the last one for which the people were to journey to Jerusalem.

"Three times a year you are to celebrate a festival to me...Celebrate the Feast of Ingathering at the end of the year when you gather in your crops from the field. Three times a year all the men are to appear before the Sovereign YHWH." (Exodus 23:14,16-17)

"Celebrate the Feast of Weeks with the first fruits of the wheat harvest, and the Feast of Ingathering in the fall of the year. Three times a year all your men are to appear before the Sovereign YHWH, the Elohim of Israel." (Exodus 34:22-23)

YHWH said to Moses, "Say to the Israelites: 'On the fifteenth day of the seventh month YHWH's feast of Tabernacles begins, and it last for seven days. The first day is a sacred assembly; do no regular work. For seven days present offerings made to YHWH by fire, and on the eighth day hold a sacred assembly; do no regular work.

" ' So beginning with the fifteenth day of the seventh month, after you have gathered the crops of the land, celebrate the festival to YHWH for seven days; the first day is a day of rest, and the eighth day also is a day of rest. On the first day you are to take choice fruit from the trees and palm fronds, leafy branches and poplars, and rejoice before YHWH your Elohim for seven days. Celebrate this as a festival to YHWH for seven days each year. This is to be a lasting ordinance for the generations to come; celebrate it in the seventh month. Live in booths for seven days; All native-born Israelites are to live in booths so your descendants will know that I had the Israelites live in booths when I brought them out of Egypt. I am YHWH your Elohim.' " (Leviticus 23:33-43)

This feast was to take place on the fifteenth day of the seventh month. It was to be a celebration of what YHWH had provided that year. It was and is also a memorial for the time the Israelites lived in tents in the wilderness before entering the Promised Land. Why would YHWH want His people to remember their time of living in tents? I think the answer to that one lies in Deuteronomy.

"Remember how YHWH your Elohim led you all the way in the desert these forty years, to humble you and to test you in order to know what was in your heart, whether or not you would keep His commands. He humbled you, causing you to hunger and then feeding you with manna, which neither you nor your fathers had known, to teach you that man does not live on bread alone, but on every word that comes from the mouth of YHWH. Your clothes did not wear out and your feet did not swell during those forty years. Know then in your heart that as a man disciplines his son; so YHWH your Elohim disciplines you." (Deuteronomy 8:2-5)

I believe that it is not only a time of remembering how YHWH provided everything His people needed while wandering in the desert, but also a form of discipline for His people. Because He loves His people, He disciplines them in order to shape them into a people who reflect His character and holiness. These are the things we are to remember as we live in tents for seven days.

"Celebrate the Feast of Tabernacles for seven days after you have gathered the produce of your threshing floor and your winepresses. Be joyful at your Feast- you, your sons and daughters, your menservants and maidservants, and the Levites and the aliens, the fatherless and the widows who live in your towns. For seven days celebrate the Feast to YHWH your Elohim at the place YHWH will choose. For YHWH your Elohim will bless you in all your harvest and in all the work of your hands, and your joy will be complete. Three times a year all your men must appear before YHWH your Elohim at the place He will choose; at the Feast of Unleavened Bread, the Feast of Weeks, and the Feast of Tabernacles. No man should appear before YHWH empty handed; Each of you must bring a gift in proportion to the way YHWH your Elohim has blessed you." (Deuteronomy 16:13-17)

Then Moses commanded them:" At the end of every seven years, in the year for canceling debts, during the Feast of Tabernacles, when all Israel comes to appear before YHWH your Elohim at the place He will choose, you shall read this law before them in their hearing. Assemble the people- men, women and children, and the aliens living in your towns- so they can listen and learn to fear YHWH your Elohim and follow carefully all the words of this law. " (Deuteronomy 31:9-12)

The instructions for celebrating the Feast of Tabernacles were:

1. Meet in the city where the tabernacle/temple was located

2. Bring palms, choice fruit, and leafy branches to celebrate before YHWH
3. Rest on the first and eighth day- no regular work
4. Live in a tent for seven days
5. This is to begin on the 15th day of the 7th month
6. Remember the time YHWH had the Israelites live in tents
7. Celebrate the harvest YHWH had given and His provision during the year
8. Bring an offering to YHWH at the tabernacle or the temple
9. Everyone was to celebrate
10. Read the whole Torah in presence of all people every seven years

YHWH specifically mentioned that everyone is supposed to celebrate this feast. No one is to be left out of the celebration. However, traveling to another city and living for seven days there could cost a lot of money. Many would be poor, or fail to plan financially, and would not have the funds to just pick up and join in on the celebration. YHWH knew this and apparently did not want anyone to miss out on the celebration due to lack of funds.

"Be sure to set aside a tenth of all that your fields produce each year. Eat the tithe of your grain, new wine and oil, and the firstborn of your herds and flocks in the presence of YHWH your Elohim at the place He will choose as a dwelling for His Name, so that you may learn to revere YHWH your Elohim always. But if that place is too distant and you have been blessed by YHWH your Elohim and cannot carry your tithe because the place where YHWH will choose to put His Name is so far away, then exchange your tithe for silver and take it with you and go to the place YHWH your Elohim will choose. Use the silver to buy whatever you like' cattle, sheep, wine or other fermented drink, or anything you wish. Then you and your household shall eat there in the presence of YHWH your Elohim and rejoice. And do not neglect the Levites living in your towns, for they have not allotment or inheritance of their own." (Deuteronomy 14:22-27)

YHWH commanded that each family set aside a tithe to provide the means necessary to purchase all that would be needed for the week-long celebrations of both Unleavened Bread and Feast of Tabernacles. He also instructed that each family was to make sure that the Levites and poor had help with whatever they might need if their tithe was not enough to cover their celebration of these feasts. YHWH wanted everyone to be celebrating before Him!

This feast points to Yeshua in several exciting ways! In John 1:14 we are told that Yeshua took on a temporary shelter (flesh) in order to sukkot (tabernacle) with us. Peter also uses the illustration of a tent to describe our earthly, temporary bodies (2 Peter 1:12-19). One day we will exchange them for an immortal body!

Yeshua observed the Feast of Tabernacles. John recorded for us that Yeshua spent time during that feast teaching in the temple courtyards. Several times in his teaching at this feast he revealed his fulfillment of scripture as the Messiah. He also promised the Holy Spirit (streams of living water) to those who would believe and follow him.

"On the last and greatest day of the Feast, Yeshua stood and said in a loud voice, 'If anyone is thirsty, let him come to me and drink. Whoever believes in me, as the scripture has said, streams of living water will flow from within him.' By this he meant the Spirit, whom those who believed in him were later to receive." (John 7:37-38)

On the eighth day of the feast Yeshua was speaking those words found in John 7. At the time He was speaking them, it is very possible the high priest was pouring a water and wine libation upon the altar as recorded by historians who witnessed these temple rituals. Later, when Yeshua died upon the cross, he was pierced in the side and out of him flowed both water and blood. This was symbolic of the living water that cleanses us and the blood that atones for us.

This feast foreshadows the thousand-year reign when our Messiah returns to this earth. We may not be living in tents during his reign here on earth, but we will be living in close communities and taking care of each other. Sukkot is definitely a rehearsal of that very thing!

We also find out from the prophet Zachariah that this feast will be celebrated every year during the reign of our Messiah. Those who do not go to celebrate the feast will be punished with lack of rain on their nations (Zachariah 14:16-19). It will be his wedding feast once his Bride is ready for the wedding at the end of the thousand-year reign (Isaiah 62:5). It also points us toward the day that YHWH will come from the heavens and dwell with man for eternity (Revelation 21:1-4).

So, we do not have a temple to approach and bring our gifts, but what can we be doing to celebrate this feast?

1. Tithe all year in preparation
2. This is to be the 15th day of the 7th month (late

September/October)
3. Bring choice fruit, leafy branches, and palms to wave before YHWH in praise
4. Meet with YHWH and celebrate with a community of believers all that YHWH has provided during the year, even His discipline to those He loves
5. Live in a tent or temporary shelter for seven days
6. Remember how YHWH made our forefathers live in tents in the wilderness
7. Rehearse the future kingdom and community living
8. Rest on the first and eighth day with a holy assembly with other believers each day
9. Bring an offering or use that offering to help others celebrate the feast
10. Make sure that all are able to celebrate
11. Read the entire Torah to the assembly every seven years

Our family has celebrated with large groups and with small groups. We have also had a few years when health or an emergency has prevented us from celebrating with a community. Those particular years we set up our tent in the backyard and slept in it during the week. One year we were fortunate to find a few other families who had also not been able to leave town, and we met with them for the sabbaths of the first day and eighth day. However, those years did not have the same joy that we experienced when we were with a community of believers all week.

Be sure that you tithe all year in preparation for this feast. Seek out a congregation or other place that may be hosting a feast and join them. There are many that are very affordably priced. These will allow you to put more of your tithe into supplies, travel, and helping others. If you cannot find one reasonably close to you, suggest to your congregation that you all camp out together at a location near you. Then, spread the word that others are welcome.

Whether you camp out with a large group or a small group, be sure that you are spending that time in celebration with a community of like-minded believers. You and your family will be richly blessed for it. It is an amazing time together with YHWH and with His people! Hallelu Yah!

Chapter 9

Hanukkah and Purim
YHWH only instructed the keeping of seven yearly holy appointed times. Those times include Passover, Unleavened Bread, First Fruits, Shavuot, Trumpets, Atonements, and Sukkot. Nevertheless, every time I speak to a group or person about the feasts of YHWH, someone will always bring up the question, "What about Hanukkah and Purim?"

Hanukkah and Purim are NOT part of YHWH's feasts or holy days. He did not command anything in regard to either of those days. They were days established by men. So, should we celebrate them?

There are groups that absolutely will not celebrate any holiday outside of YHWH's feasts. This includes religious and secular holidays. They rightfully do not celebrate Christmas, but neither do they celebrate Thanksgiving or Independence Day. Those people would not celebrate Hanukkah or Purim, either.

I always prefer to return to what YHWH said. After all, it is Him that we claim to love, obey, and represent. And it is by His words that we live. Let's take a look at His words concerning festivals outside of His holy days.

YHWH said to Moses, "Speak to the Israelites and say to them; 'I am YHWH your Elohim. You must not do as they do in Egypt, where you used to live, and you must not do as they do in the land of Canaan, where I am brining you. Do not follow their practices. You must obey my laws and be careful to follow my decrees. I am YHWH your Elohim. Keep my decrees and laws, for the man who obeys them will live by them. I am YHWH.'" (Leviticus 18:1-5)

"Destroy completely all the places on the high mountains and on the hills and under every spreading tree where the nations you are dispossessing worship their gods. Break down their altars, smash their sacred stones and burn their Asherah poles in the fire, cut down the idols of their gods and wipe out their names from those places. You must not worship YHWH your Elohim in the ways of the pagans." (Deuteronomy 12:2-4)

Be careful not to be ensnared by inquiring about their gods, saying, "How do these nations serve their gods?" We will do the same," You must not worship YHWH your Elohim in their way, because in worshiping their gods they do all kinds of detestable things YHWH hates. They even burn their sons and daughters in the fire as sacrifices to their gods." (Deuteronomy 12:30-32)

These and many more verses tell us that YHWH does not want us participating in any activity or practice that the pagans incorporate in the worship of their false gods. He especially does not want us worshipping Him in the ways of the pagans. Even something as simple as dying eggs is not to be done by YHWH's people because it is part of fertility rituals done by pagans in the worship of their fertility goddess. Putting gifts under a tree was done to appease the sun gods. Those gifts were usually sacrificed children. Kissing under the mistletoe was to ensure fertility of the womb. Jack-o-lanterns and trick or treating were practices involved in the worship of ancestors and the dead.

However, there is nothing in scripture that tells us not to participate in things that are secular that are not related to worship of false gods. This would include things such as a holiday to celebrate the establishment of a country, as long as the activities involved are not related to false religious activities.

So, then we have to look at what are Hanukkah and Purim?

- What is being celebrated?
- Why is it being celebrated?
- How is it being celebrated?
- Does it honor YHWH?

The fourth question is the greatest question since you bear His Name, and we are not to take His Name in vain. If you are participating in something that defiles or dishonors Him, then of course it takes His Name in vain and should not be a part of your life. We are to be separate from, not similar to, the world.

Let's look at these two holidays. We will start with Hanukkah. This feast is usually in the month we call December. According to the Hebrew calendar it falls on the 25th day of the 9th month. Why? What happened? To keep this as short as possible I am going to just give you the highlights of what happened. You can find out more in your own search in history and in the book of Daniel where these things were prophesied hundreds of years before they happened.

In 170 BC there was a king that controlled much of what we would consider today to be Turkey, Syria, Iraq, Iran, Afghanistan, Pakistan, and India. His name was Antiochus IV. He was considered by his own people to be a madman. He thought that he was the earthly manifestation of his god. He greatly desired to take over the Ptolemaic Empire that consisted of what is today Israel and Egypt.

Under the Ptolemaic Empire, the Jews did well. They were treated well, allowed to move about the empire freely, and allowed to practice their beliefs freely. Once Antiochus IV started wars with Ptolemy things for the Jews changed. Antiochus had to march through Israel to get to Egypt. Along the way he took Jewish cities and posted his army in them.

Antiochus IV outlawed the practice of reading the Torah and burned all the copies he could find. If someone was found to have the Torah, that person was usually burned to death. He outlawed the practice of circumcision. If a baby was found to be circumcised, the baby was killed and hung around the mother's neck as the soldiers made her parade through the town until they killed her. All religious practices of the Jews were also outlawed. The eating of pork and the worship of Antiochus and his god Zeus were forced upon the Jews. Those Jews who refused were killed.

After a rather humiliating defeat against Ptolemy in the 6th Syrian war, Antiochus came back through Israel and set up an image of himself in the most holy place of the temple in Jerusalem. He then had pigs sacrificed to him and to Zeus on the altar in the temple. He further defiled the temple by allowing prostitution to occur within YHWH's temple. Those things had been prophesied by Daniel hundreds of years before they happened (Daniel 8:9-12; 11:21-45).

It was during this particular event that a small group of Jews who were led by a man named Matthias fled to the mountains. There the men gathered around Matthias and his five sons. They began an attack on the Syrian army. They would come out of the mountains, attack fast and hard, then disappear back into the mountains. This form of attack led to the men being called the Maccabeus, Hebrew for hammer.

After three and a half years of this war against the Syrian army in Jerusalem, the Maccabeus finally took back the city and temple. They cleaned out the temple. They destroyed the defiled altar, built a new one, and dedicated the new altar. Judah Maccabeus declared that all generations should forever remember the dedication of the altar on the 25th of Kislev (ninth month) of every year.

Unfortunately, the Maccabeus took liberties with YHWH's instructions. They dedicated the altar for eight days instead of seven. They also celebrated the Feast of Sukkot at that time. Scripture tells us specifically that the altar is to be dedicated for seven days, not eight, and Sukkot is to be celebrated in the seventh month, not the ninth (Exodus 29:37; Leviticus 23:34).

You can find this story in the books of Maccabees, particularly book one and two. They decided to forever commemorate the day that the altar was dedicated to YHWH after their war with Antiochus IV. Hanukkah specifically means "dedication". This was to be the reason for celebrating this holiday each year.

Years after Yeshua was resurrected, the rabbis began adding to the actual historical facts. They stated that when the Maccabeus dedicated the altar there was only enough oil for the Menorah to burn one day, but by a miracle, the oil lasted eight days. That is why today, Hanukkah is also called the Festival of Lights. However, there is not any written documentation of this miracle before Yeshua's time, specifically no mention of it by the very people who supposedly witnessed this miracle, the Maccabeus. The Maccabeus made it clear they were celebrating the dedication of the new altar. They did not call for a holiday to celebrate a miracle of oil.

Today, many Jews celebrate Hanukkah as a memorial to the rabbinically declared miracle of oil they say lasted for eight days. They light candles in a hanukkiah that looks like a nine-branched menorah. YHWH made it clear to Moses that the furnishings of the tabernacle were to be according to the pattern show to him from the heavens (Exodus 25:9, 40). That command included the menorah, the lampstand within the holy place of the tabernacle and temple. That pattern given for the menorah was a seven-branched lampstand. The hanukkiah is essentially the menorah with two added branches.

Other traditions include frying latkes (potato pancakes), eating dairy, playing games with chocolate "gold coins" and giving gifts all eight nights. Some Jews even have a Hanukkah bush, under which they place their gifts. There is even a Hanukkah Harry who is dressed in a blue and white outfit similar to the red one worn by Santa Claus. None of these traditions have anything to do with the dedication of the altar. They seem a lot like a substitute for those who do not celebrate Christmas.

Am I saying that one should not celebrate Hanukkah? In the couple of decades that our family has been walking this path with YHWH, only once has He laid it on my heart for our family to celebrate the holiday. Our celebration consisted of seven nights of discussing the lives of people who stood firm in their convictions regarding YHWH and obeying His instructions no matter what the outcome might bring. We discussed the prophets, Maccabeus, the apostles, as well as many of the martyrs from AD 300 to present day. Dedicating our hearts to YHWH was the other topic discussed each night. It looked nothing like a typical Hanukkah celebration.

I do not presume to tell people whether or not they should celebrate Hanukkah. I simply encourage them to know the facts. Then, answer for themselves the questions that I asked at the beginning of this chapter.

- What am I celebrating?
- Why am I celebrating?
- How am I celebrating?
- Does this honor YHWH?

If you are wanting to have a party and invite people over for some fun, there is nothing that says you have to wait till a "declared holiday" to do so. YHWH's people are encouraged to rejoice always (Psalm 32:11; Philippians 4:4)!

The other widely celebrated holiday outside of YHWH's Feasts is Purim. Purim is found in the book of Esther. Queen Esther and Mordecai worked together to save the Jews from destruction during the Persian Empire, an event that took place hundreds of years before the Maccabeus.

Mordecai worked for the King of Persia. He had a position of high honor in the king's court. However, he refused to bow before any man, including Haman who was higher in honor in the king's court. Haman came from a long line of haters of Israel, and in fact was descended from Amalek, the grandson of Esau. The fact that Mordecai refused to bow to him made Haman bitter toward all Jews. So, he tricked the king into letting him declare war upon the Jews with the intent of destroying them completely. By casting lots he had determined the day to do that would be on the 13th day of the 12th month, which on our calendar is called late February to late March.

Mordecai appealed to Esther to approach the king and seek to intercede on behalf of the Jews. Esther knew that to appear before the king without invitation could mean one's immediate death. However, after fasting and praying for three days, she dressed in her finest and dared to approach the king. YHWH obviously caused the king to look upon Esther with favor and the king allowed her to make her request. She invited the king and Haman to a banquet.

On the second day of the banquet the king offered Queen Esther anything she desired. She asked him to save her people. She informed him of Haman's plot to kill all the Jews. The king became angry at the deceit and the threat to his own queen's life. He had Haman killed and told Mordecai to write a decree allowing all the Jews to take up arms and defend themselves on the 13th day of the 12th month.

When the 13th day of the 12th month arrived, the Jews defended themselves, but did not deliberately kill anyone, nor did they take any spoils from those who were killed. This success moved Mordecai to declare that the 14th day of the 12th month be held as a day of celebration for all Jews of all generations. They were celebrating their deliverance from an ancient enemy. This is the reason for the celebration. Purim was the word for "lots" that were cast for Haman to determine the day he would annihilate the Jews.

Today, Purim is celebrated by many who make it look similar to Halloween and Mardi Gras. The kids dress up in costumes, presumably to pretend to be Mordecai and Esther or the King of Persia. However, there are too many who are dressing up as many other things not remotely related to the purpose of Purim. There are many, even in Israel, who take this opportunity to cross dress. There is lots of candy and even games such as bobbing for apples and beads worn or thrown to others just like in Mardi Gras. Many will read through the book of Esther and have the kids participate with "boo's", "hooray's", and other such noises to praise the names of Esther and Mordecai and to "blot" out the name of Haman.

It is obvious that this was not how the day of Purim was originally celebrated. Should you celebrate Purim? It is always good to read through the book of Esther, but you shouldn't have to wait for a holiday to do that. It is good to celebrate with YHWH's people the deliverance from destruction, but again, you shouldn't have to wait for a holiday to do that. As to the rest of it? Again, I go back to the questions asked earlier.

- What am I celebrating?
- Why am I celebrating?
- How am I celebrating?
- Is what I am doing honor YHWH?

Since these are not holy days commanded by YHWH, it is not sin for anyone to refuse to celebrate them. However, since the days themselves are not a Christianized form of pagan worship days, it is not a sin for anyone to participate in the day of celebration. One must be sure that what one does in celebration is not related to pagan worship nor brings dishonor to YHWH. YHWH's people are never to adopt the rituals of paganism or to look like those who do those things. Do not compromise with the world. Keep your celebrations separate from those of the world and be sure that they truly honor YHWH in a way that is acceptable to Him.

These are two instances where one must use discernment and listen to the voice of our Shepherd as one decides What am I celebrating? Why am I celebrating? How am I celebrating? Is what I am doing honor YHWH?

May your ears be attuned to what YHWH desires for you, your family, and your congregation. Blessings and shalom!

Chapter 10

Conclusion

"Therefore, do not let anyone judge you by what you eat or drink, or with regard to the feasts, a new moon celebration, or the Sabbath. These are a shadow of the things that are to come; the reality, now is found in Messiah." Colossians 2:18

Paul was writing to believers who had been former gentiles. They had chosen to leave the ways of the pagans for the ways of YHWH. They were looking very different from their pagan neighbors and family members. They were also facing pressure from certain Jews to convert to Judaism and celebrate the feasts according to the Pharisaic traditions. Changing the feasts they celebrated from the ones of their pagan upbringing to the ones YHWH instructed for those who became His redeemed people was not easy.

Paul (Shaul) wanted to encourage these believers to continue in what they were learning from scripture; to stand against opposition. He encouraged them to go forward in what YHWH instructed instead of looking to man-made traditions. He also encouraged them to remember that it all points to our Messiah and the prophecies about Him; the ones fulfilled and the ones that have yet to be fulfilled.

I felt there could be no better ending to this book. As you start walking in the instructions of our God in celebrating His feasts and holy days I pray that you will be encouraged to go forward, even in the midst of pressures from loved ones who do not choose to do the same or celebrate using pagan ways. I pray that you will remember that YHWH gave us all the instruction we need for celebrating each one. We do not have to look to man-made traditions to understand or to properly celebrate the feasts. Most importantly, remember that each one speaks of our Messiah and His work of reconciling us to our God and Creator.

May YHWH bless and guide you as you prove faithful with each feast He has given us to celebrate. Hallelu Yah!

• • • •

THANK YOU FOR READING my book. If you enjoyed it, won't you please take a moment to leave me a review at your favorite retailer?

Would you like to learn more? Visit my site: Seven Lamps Ministries[1]

Thank you!

DeAnna

---

1. http://www.sevenlampsministries.com/

www.ingramcontent.com/pod-product-compliance
Lightning Source LLC
Chambersburg PA
CBHW032150040426
42449CB00005B/463